AF605672

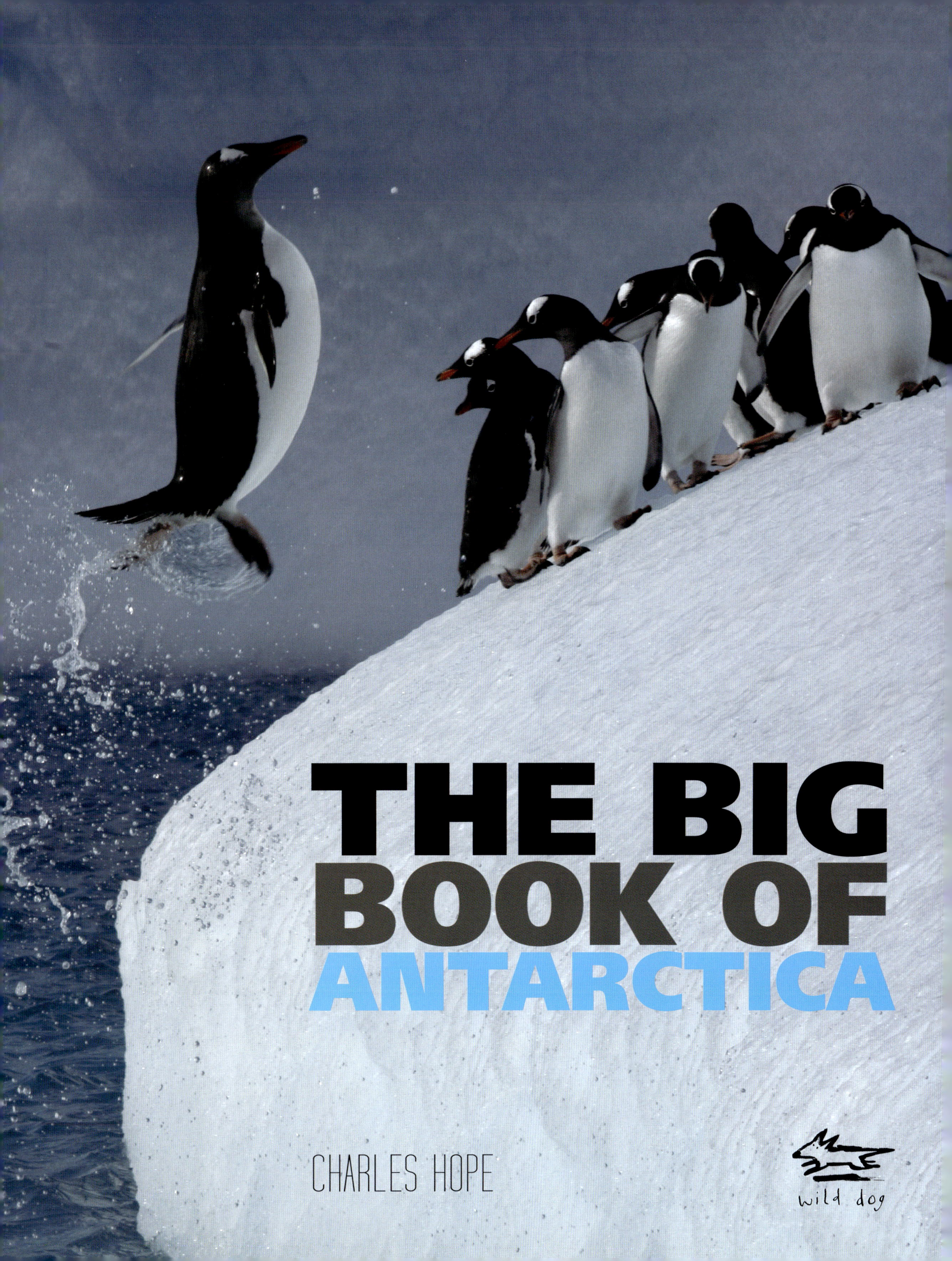

THE BIG BOOK OF ANTARCTICA

CHARLES HOPE

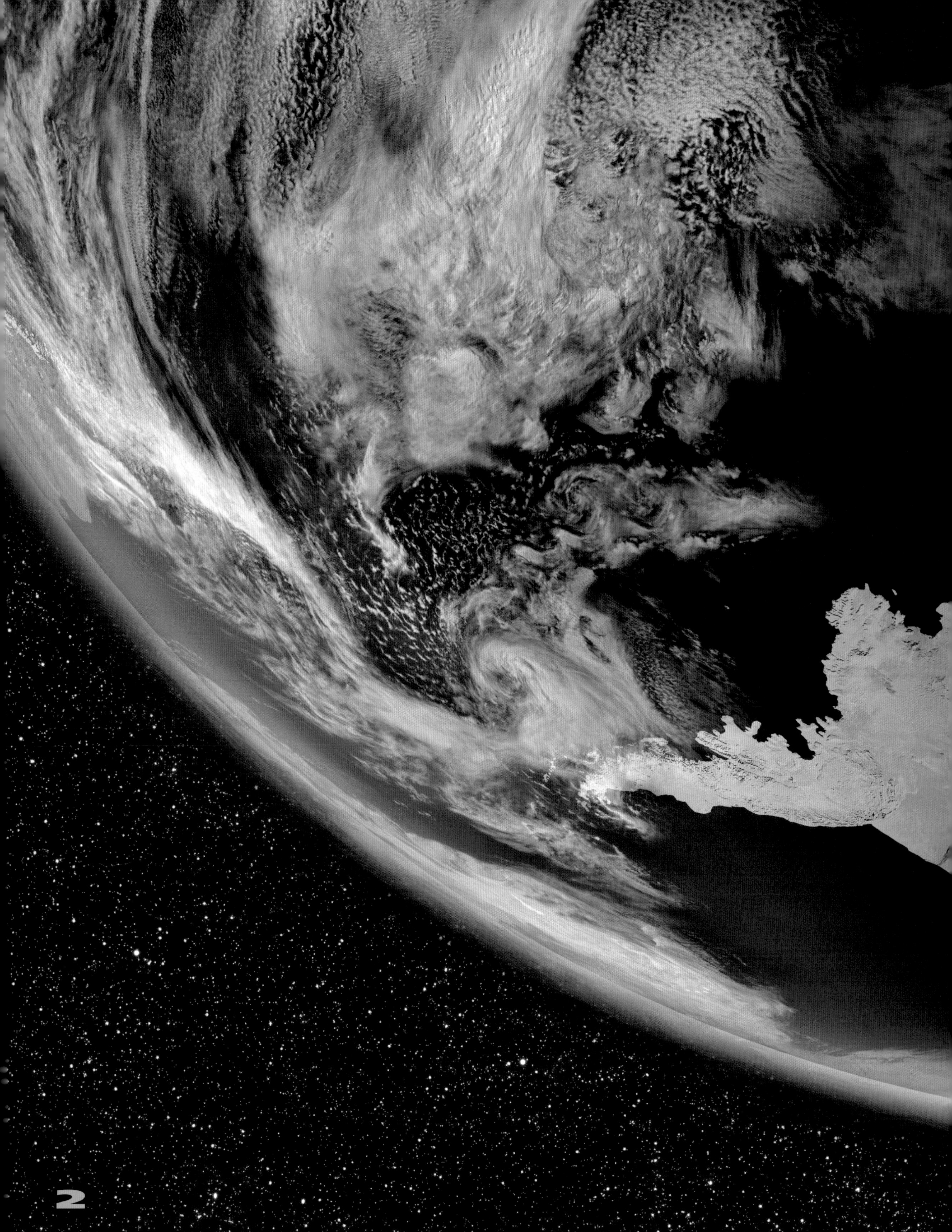

ANTARCTICA

is at the south of the Earth. It is the fifth-largest continent, and the last to be discovered by humans.

Antarctica is the driest, coldest, highest and windiest continent on Earth. Most of the landscape is barren, lifeless

DESERT.

Despite the harsh conditions, Antarctica is bursting with **LIFE**.

It supports a wide range of living creatures, and many of these come back to Antarctica to breed.

Antarctica is a long way from the rest of the world. The countries closest to it are **ARGENTINA**, **CHILE**, **NEW ZEALAND** and **AUSTRALIA**.

The continent of Antarctica has an area of close to **14 MILLION SQUARE KILOMETRES**. This area includes some of the surrounding islands. It also includes many ice shelves, such as Ronne and Ross, which are massive sheets of fresh-water ice that float on the ocean and are attached to the ice sheet covering Antarctica.

During the winter months, large amounts of

SEA ICE

form around the Antarctic continent. As much as 20 million square kilometres is created, which drops down to about two million square kilometres during the warmer months. Sea ice is very important to some Antarctic animals, such as emperor and Adélie penguins. Emperors breed on sea ice, while Adélies need to cross it to reach their nests.

The idea of Antarctica's existence was first suggested by the ancient Greeks several thousand years before it was discovered. A number of people came close to finding it, including Captain James Cook in 1773. The first people to actually see Antarctica were **FABIAN GOTTLIEB VON BELLINGSHAUSEN**, **EDWARD BRANSFIELD** and **NATHANIEL PALMER**. These three men all saw the mainland of Antarctica on separate occasions, and ships, sometime in early 1820.

Many famous adventurers have explored Antarctica. One of them was the Australian

DOUGLAS MAWSON.

He was a member of Ernest Shackleton's expedition of 1907–09, and later led his own expedition in 1911–14. This later mission was the first to use radio communications in Antarctica.

The first person to reach the South Pole was

ROALD AMUNDSEN.

This Norwegian explorer and his team arrived at the pole just one month ahead of their rivals.

A month after Amundsen, a second expedition led by the Englishman **ROBERT FALCON SCOTT** arrived at the South Pole. Knowing they had been beaten, the five-man team attempted to return to their base but none of them survived.

One of the most famous explorers of Antarctica was the Irishman **ERNEST SHACKLETON**. After two unsuccessful attempts to reach the South Pole, he tried to become the first person to travel across the continent. However, on his way there his ship became trapped in sea ice and eventually sank. What followed was one of the most celebrated stories of survival, as it wasn't until two years later his expedition was finally rescued.

Whales have been hunted by humans for thousands of years. Their meat, skin, blubber and internal organs were valuable as food, while some species of whale produced precious whale oil and whalebone. The different parts of whales were used to make a range of products such as candles, toys, soap, jewellery, clothing and margarine. Whaling crews were sailing into Antarctic waters from the mid-1700s, catching and killing any whales they could find by spearing them with **HARPOONS**.

The commercial whaling industry grew around the world during the 1800s, and by the 1900s Antarctica had become the whaling capital of the planet. South Georgia Island was home to several famous stations, such as Leith Harbour, Stromness and

GRYTVIKEN.

During its peak, this whaling station was home to 300 men as well as a church and cinema. It is also where the famous Antarctic explorer Ernest Shackleton was buried.

DECEPTION ISLAND

was home to both seal and whaling stations. When the whaling industry collapsed during the mid-1900s, this station, like many others, was abandoned.

There are usually between several hundred and a couple of thousand people living in Antarctica. More people live there during the warmer months.

SCIENTISTS

make up the majority of people living in Antarctica, and come from lots of different countries around the world.

Antarctic scientists perform experiments to help us learn more about the environment and the health of our planet. Their research includes subjects like marine biology, astronomy, geology and **CLIMATE CHANGE**.

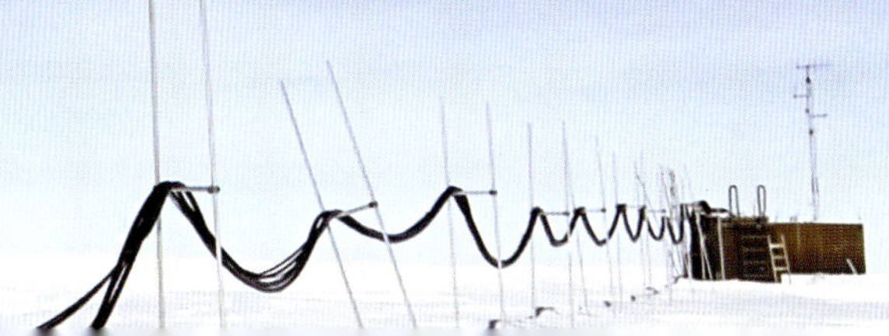

Most of the Antarctic continent – as much as 98 per cent – is covered by a **SHEET OF ICE** with an average thickness of close to two kilometres.

Despite the lack of suitable ground, a small number of plants can be found on Antarctica. This includes nearly one hundred species of **MOSS**.

Algae are simple marine plants. There are several hundred different species found in Antarctica.

SNOW ALGAE, which is also known as watermelon or blood snow, is a type of algae well suited to living in the cold.

Three types of **LICHEN** are found in Antarctica. Lichens are plants that are made up of fungi and algae.

Some of the most important organisms in Antarctica are the planktons, such as **ZOOPLANKTON**. These are tiny life forms that drift around in the ocean.

Perhaps the most important of all the planktons is **PHYTOPLANKTON**. These organisms drift near the surface, as they use sunlight to photosynthesise. Phytoplankton is a central part of the ocean food web.

Phytoplankton and zooplankton are the preferred foods of **KRILL**.

These shrimp-like creatures are an important food source for a range of marine animals. Without krill, there would be much less life in Antarctica.

KING PENGUINS

are relatively large and can be recognised by the golden-orange feathers on their necks. They range as far north as South Africa and Australia, though spend much of their time on the rocky subantarctic islands, where they live and breed in large colonies. While both parents look after their newborns, older chicks go to penguin 'kinders' where they are guarded by only a few adults. This gives the other adults a chance to get some food.

WEDDELL SEALS

spend most of their life either on or under the Antarctic ice. This helps keep them safe from predators like killer whales. They enter and exit the water through breathing holes, which they manage to keep open by scraping at them with their teeth. Weddell seals dive to depths of 600 metres for fish, squid and krill, and can find their way back to their breathing holes by using echolocation and their excellent eyesight.

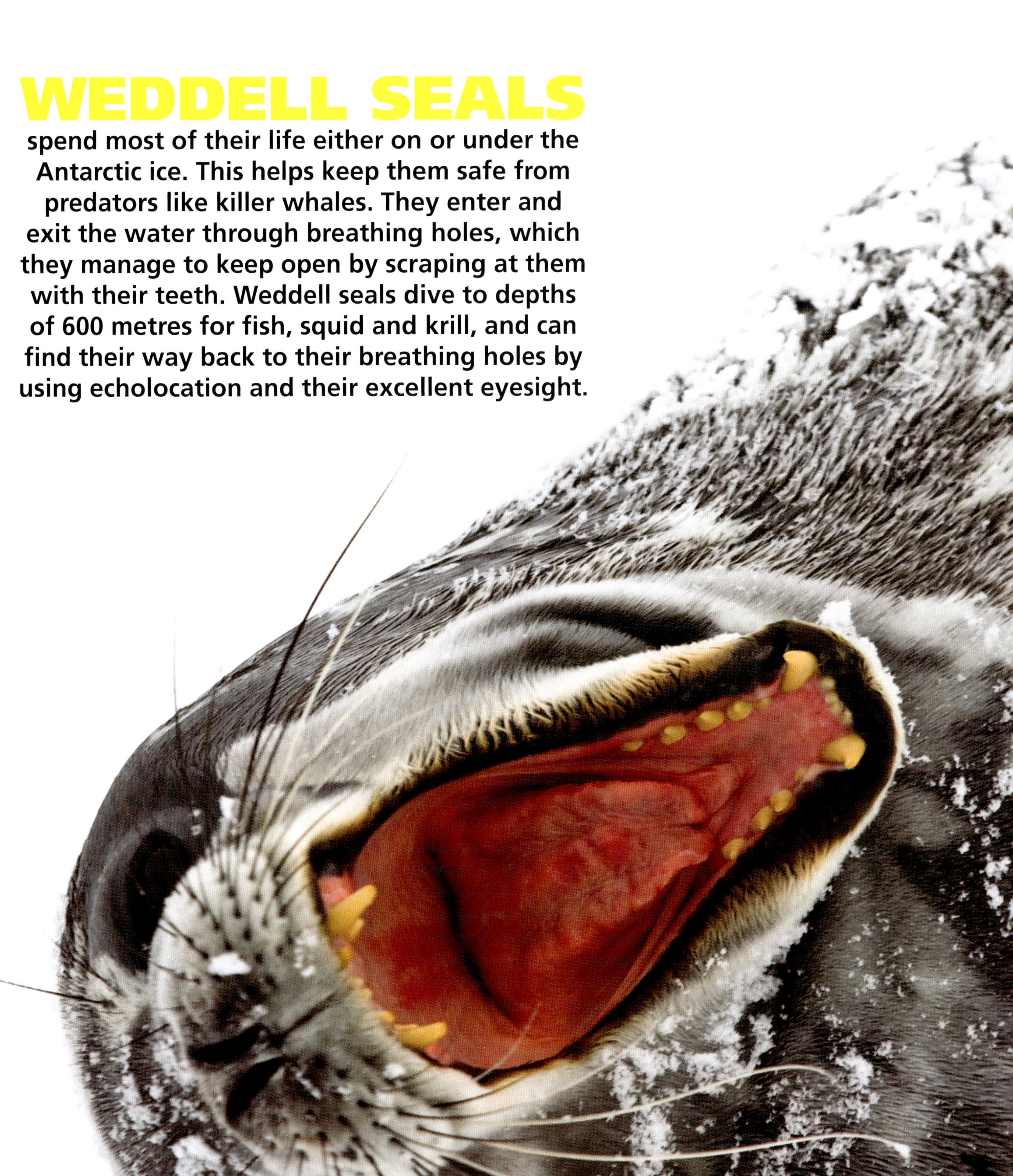

SNOWY SHEATHBILLS

are the only land birds native to Antarctica. These scavengers survive by eating anything they can get their beaks on. This includes stealing (fish and krill from penguins, or penguin eggs and chicks), eating carrion (the rotten flesh of dead animals) and looking through faeces for undigested food.

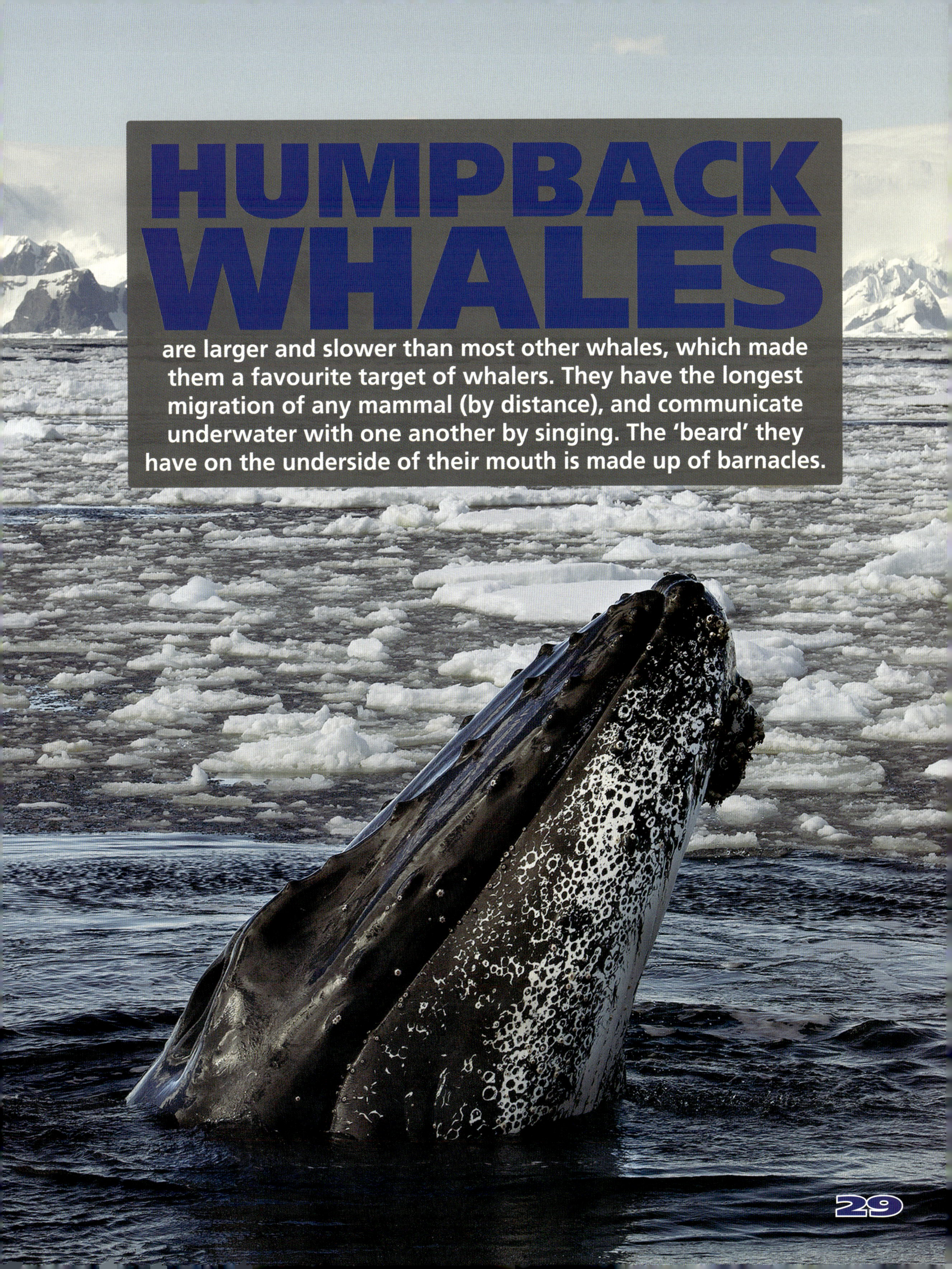

HUMPBACK WHALES

are larger and slower than most other whales, which made them a favourite target of whalers. They have the longest migration of any mammal (by distance), and communicate underwater with one another by singing. The 'beard' they have on the underside of their mouth is made up of barnacles.

ANTARCTIC FUR SEALS

are close relatives of the dog. A thick layer of fur keeps them warm, unlike other Antarctic seals, which rely on their fat stores to stay alive. Male fur seals are much bigger than females, and during mating season become jealous, aggressive and violent towards other males. They act like this in an attempt to keep females for themselves.

BROWN SKUAS

can be found across the Southern Hemisphere, from New Zealand to South America, and South Africa to Australia. When it is time to breed, they travel south towards Antarctica and the subantarctic islands, where they often nest close to penguin colonies. Much of their diet comes from unguarded penguin eggs and chicks, though they also eat fish, crustaceans and other seabirds.

LEOPARD SEALS

are fearsome ocean predators. Though they are heavy – females can weigh close to 600 kilograms – they are fast and deadly hunters that like to eat fish, seals and penguins. They sometimes 'play' with their victims, chasing them away from land until their prey become exhausted and give up.

CHINSTRAP PENGUINS

are social creatures that communicate with one another by bowing, grooming themselves and waving their heads and flippers. When they become angry, their gestures change to pointing, staring and even charging at their enemies. These small penguins can be easily identified by the line of black feathers under their chins. Their predators include orcas, sharks and leopard seals.

WANDERING ALBATROSSES

are seabirds that breed in pairs for life. Adults produce only one egg every two years, if not longer. They spend most of their lives in the air, and only come to ground for food and nesting.

GENTOO PENGUINS

use stones to build their nests, placing them in a pile in the shape of a circle. Good quality stones are valuable items in Gentoo colonies and fiercely guarded. Because of this they build their nests more than two 'attack lengths' apart, so that neighbouring penguins aren't constantly pecking at one another.

CRABEATER SEALS

do not eat crabs. Instead, they mostly eat krill, fish and soft-bodied animals like squid and octopus. They gather in groups when they are young and become solitary as they get older. Crabeaters are preyed on by leopard seals and killer whales, though their numbers are incredibly healthy; after humans, they are the biggest population of large animals on the planet.

GIANT PETRELS

are scavenger birds that feed on, among other things, the carcasses of animals and the waste products of passing ships. They are also known as 'stinkers', and get this name from a defensive habit of vomiting on anything they consider to be a threat.

ADÉLIE PENGUINS

spend the warmer months on the Antarctic continent where they mate and nest before moving out to sea on the pack ice during the colder months. Like all penguins, they are strong swimmers. They are also famous for jumping, walking long distances and tobogganing across the snow on their stomachs.

ELEPHANT SEALS

are well equipped for the harsh climate of Antarctica. They have a thick layer of blubber and a huge amount of blood in their body, which allows them to dive deep and stay underwater for long periods – in some cases up to two hours.

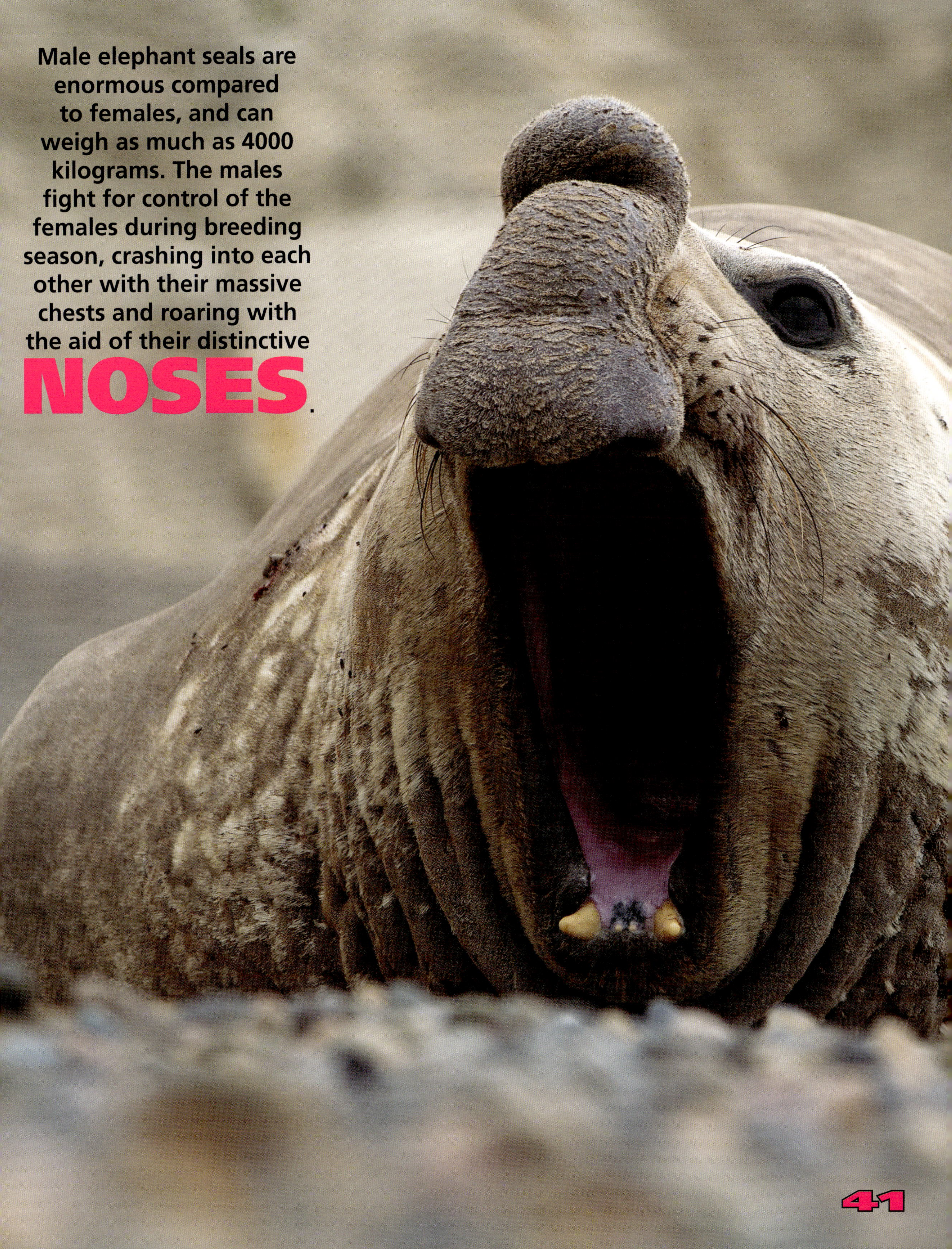

Male elephant seals are enormous compared to females, and can weigh as much as 4000 kilograms. The males fight for control of the females during breeding season, crashing into each other with their massive chests and roaring with the aid of their distinctive **NOSES**.

MACARONI PENGUINS

are found in Antarctica and its surrounding islands, and are often confused with rockhoppers (opposite). One way to tell them apart is to look at the feathers on their heads. Macaronis have crest feathers that stick out to the sides of their eyes.

ROCKHOPPER PENGUINS

have crest feathers that follow the shape of their heads, and are less spiky than those of macaronis.

IMPERIAL SHAGS

belong to the cormorant family. They are found in Antarctica and its surrounding islands, where there are several breeding colonies. Imperial shags catch fish by diving into the water. Like penguins and many other birds, shags regurgitate food for their chicks to eat.

KILLER WHALES,

also known as orcas, are found in oceans around the world. Most of them live in the waters of Antarctica. They are fearsome and intelligent predators that eat squid, fish, seals, penguins and other whales.

EMPEROR PENGUINS

are some of the best equipped animals for life in the cold. They are kept warm by multiple layers of tightly packed feathers, and when faced with extreme cold and wind they come together in large groups to save body heat. They rotate their position in the group so that everyone can stay as warm as possible.

Emperors are so well suited to the cold that they are the only animals capable of breeding during the Antarctic winter.

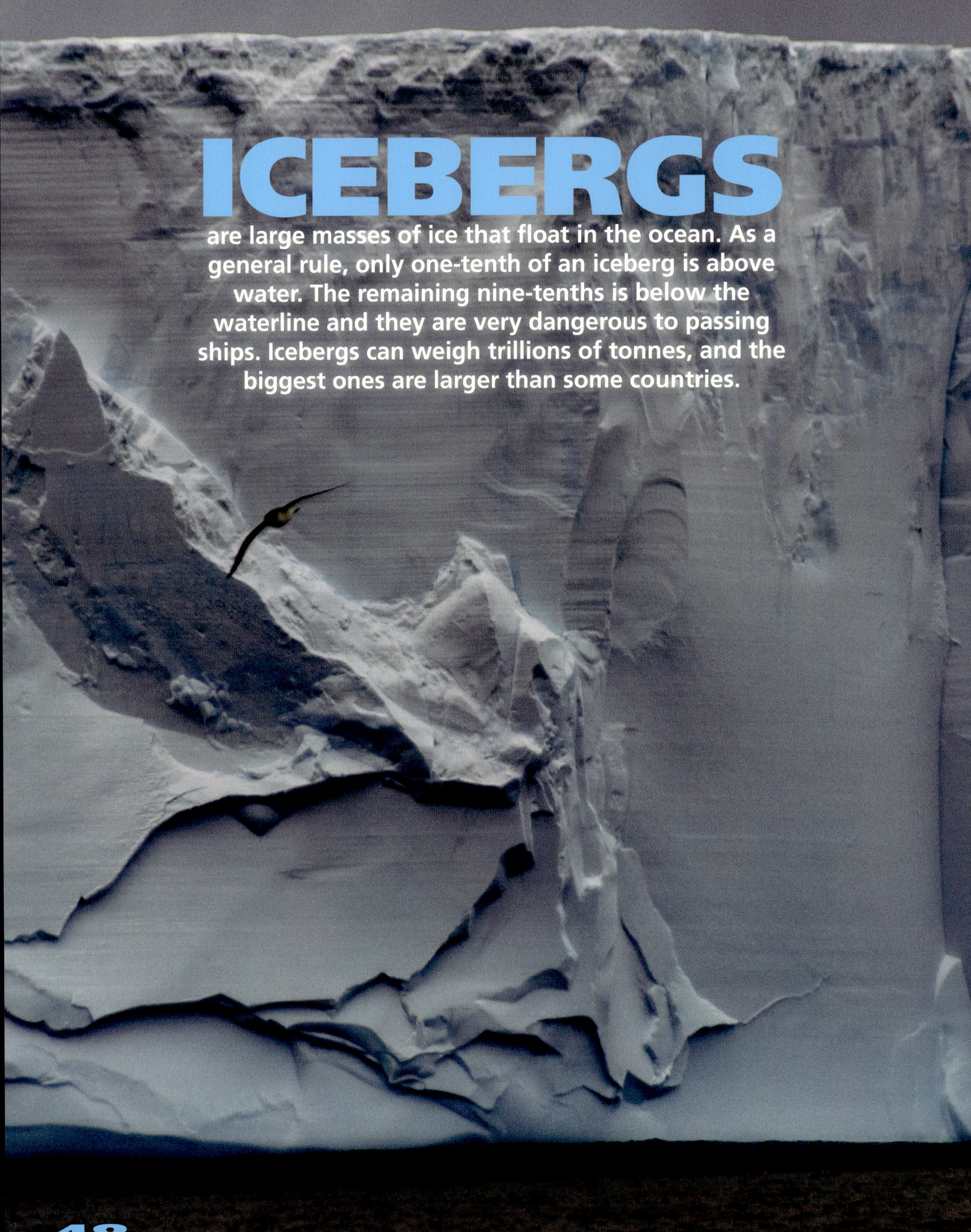

ICEBERGS

are large masses of ice that float in the ocean. As a general rule, only one-tenth of an iceberg is above water. The remaining nine-tenths is below the waterline and they are very dangerous to passing ships. Icebergs can weigh trillions of tonnes, and the biggest ones are larger than some countries.

Icebergs can be divided into two categories:

TABULAR AND NON-TABULAR.

Tabular icebergs have a flat top and steep sides, like the iceberg on the opposite page. Non-tabular icebergs have different shapes, such as dome, pinnacle and wedge.

has become increasingly popular in Antarctica, with close to 40,000 people visiting every year. There are many popular activities for tourists. These include interacting with penguins, getting close enough to touch an iceberg, wildlife spotting, visiting the South Pole and taking in the stunning beauty that makes Antarctica such a magical place to experience.

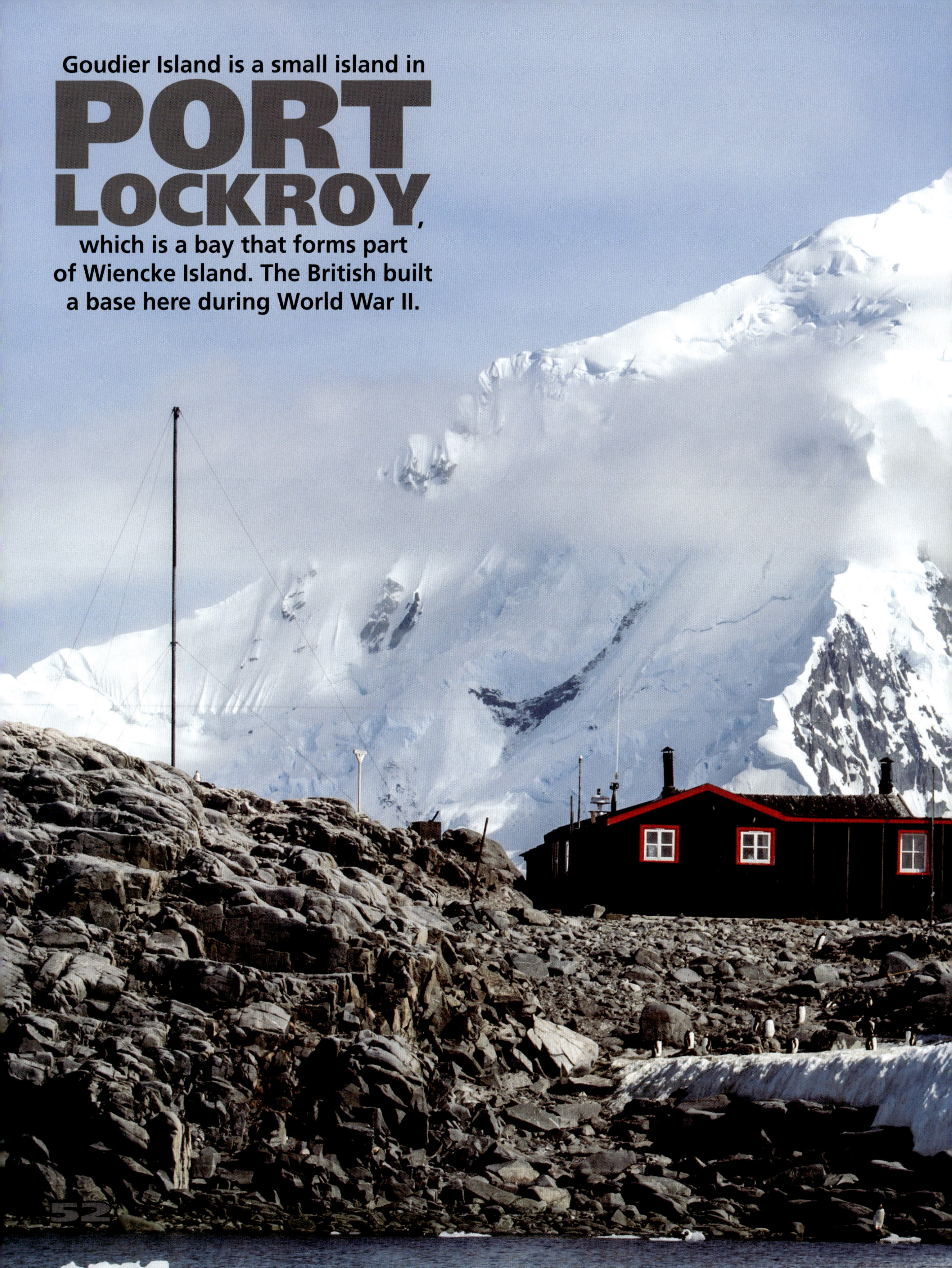

Goudier Island is a small island in **PORT LOCKROY**, which is a bay that forms part of Wiencke Island. The British built a base here during World War II.

After the war, the base was turned into a research station and eventually abandoned. During the 1990s it was reopened as a museum and post office. It is also home to a population of Gentoo penguins.

MOUNT EREBUS

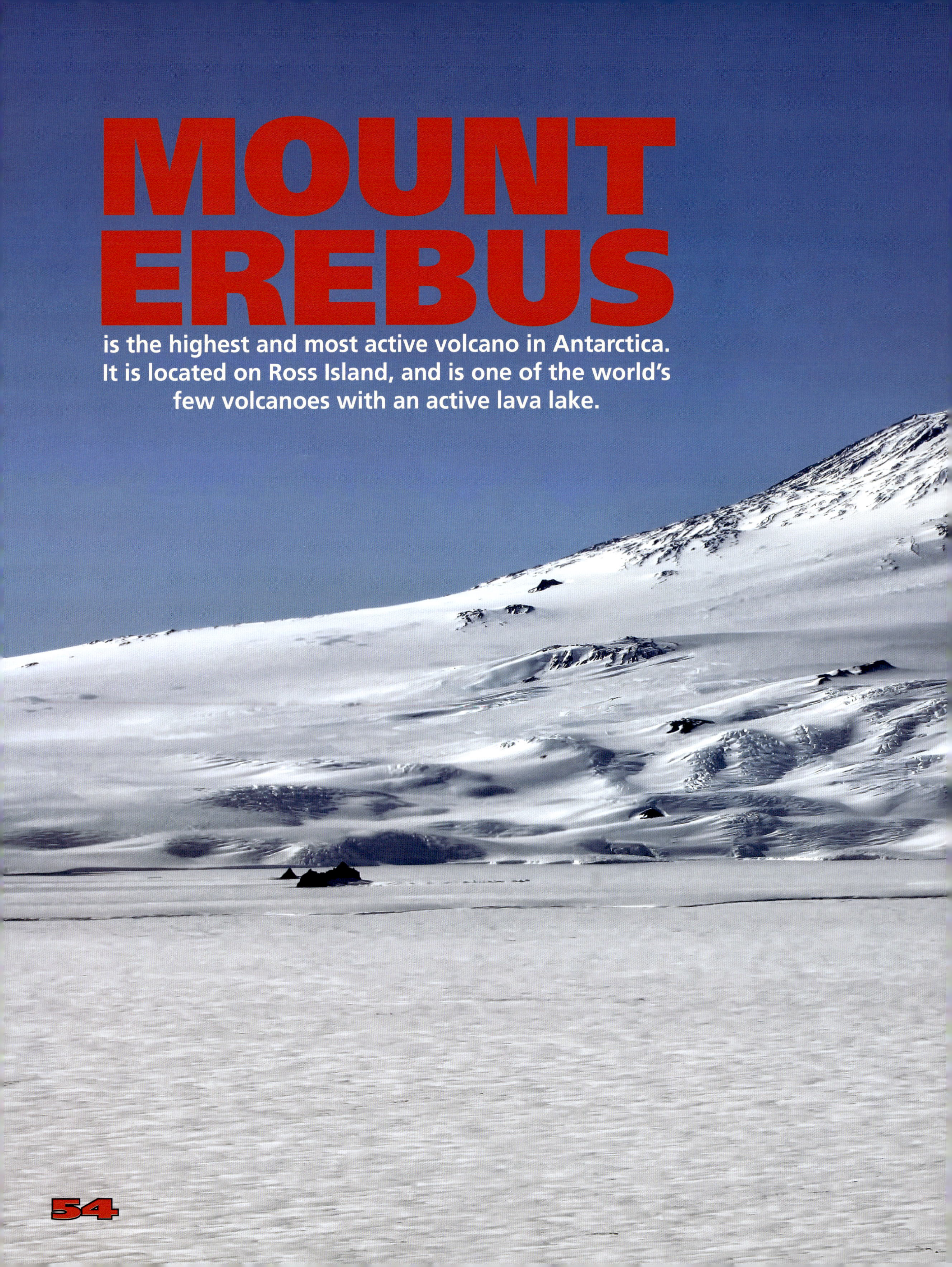

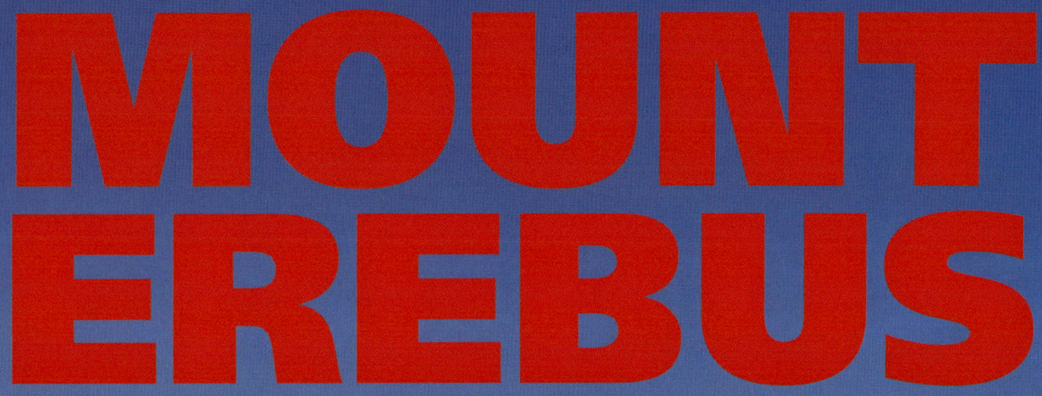

is the highest and most active volcano in Antarctica. It is located on Ross Island, and is one of the world's few volcanoes with an active lava lake.

CARGO SHIPS

are used to transport scientists and their supplies to the many research stations in Antarctica. Clear channels are needed for these ships to avoid them becoming trapped in the ice.

ICEBREAKERS

are powerful ships used to clear paths through the ice. These ships are different from others in three main ways: they have a stronger hull, a shape designed to break through ice and more power to help them push through the ice. Icebreakers are also used to rescue other ships that become trapped.

Getting to Antarctica is now much safer and easier than when the first explorers and whalers arrived.

PLANES

and helicopters are used to transport people and supplies to over 30 different airfields along the Antarctic coastline.

Antarctica is home to about 90 per cent of Earth's ice, and accounts for close to 70 per cent of the fresh water on the planet. If all this ice were to melt, the sea level around the world would rise by nearly 60 metres. As temperatures on Earth continue to increase, so too will the temperatures of our oceans. This overall

GLOBAL WARMING

will continue to cause more and more ice to break away from Antarctica and melt into the ocean. The primary cause of global warming is human activity.

GLOSSARY

ALGAE a type of marine plant.

ANCIENT very old.

ASTRONOMY the science of space and the universe.

BARNACLE a type of marine crustacean.

BARREN land that is too poor to produce much life.

BLUBBER the fat of sea mammals.

BREED to mate and produce offspring.

CARCASS the dead body of an animal.

CHANNEL a stretch of water that is safe for ships to navigate.

COLONY a group of plants or animals living together.

CONTINENT a large, continuous area of land; the seven continents of Earth are Africa, Asia, Europe, North America, South America, Australia and Antarctica.

CRUSTACEAN a type of invertebrate found mostly in the ocean, and which usually has a hard covering.

ECHOLOCATION the ability to use sounds and their echoes to navigate.

EXPEDITION journey.

FAECES poo.

FUNGUS a type of organism that feeds on organic matter.

GEOLOGY the science of Earth's physical structure.

HULL the main body of a ship, including the bottom, sides and deck.

INVERTEBRATE an animal that does not have a backbone.

MAMMAL an animal that is warm-blooded and has a backbone, among other key features.

MARINE found in the sea.

MIGRATE to move from one place to another according to the season.

NATIVE an animal that is local to a specific area.

NAVIGATE to find your way around.

PECK to strike or bite at something; usually by a bird with their beak.

PHOTOSYNTHESIS a process used by some plants and organisms where sunlight is used to make nutrients.

POPULATION number of people, animals or plants.

PREDATOR an animal that kills and eats other animals for food.

PREY an animal that is hunted and killed by another animal for food.

REGURGITATE to bring swallowed food back up and into the mouth.

SCAVENGE to search for waste items as food.

SOLITARY an animal that prefers to live by itself.

INDEX

First published in 2017 by
wild dog
54A Alexandra Parade
Clifton Hill Vic 3068
Australia
+61 3 9419 9406
dog@wdog.com.au
wdog.com.au

Printed and bound in China by 1010 Printing International

National Library of Australia
Cataloguing-in-Publication data:
Creator: Hope, Charles.
Title: The Big Book of Antarctica.
ISBN: 9781742034188 (pbk)
Target Audience: For primary school age.
Subjects: Natural history--Antarctica--Juvenile literature.
Dewey Number: 508.99

Wild Dog would like to thank Wendy Pyper (Australian Antarctic Division) for her careful fact checking and Neil Conning for his thorough proofreading.

10 9 8 7 6 5 4 3 24 25 26 27 28

PHOTO CREDITS:
Images courtesy of Shutterstock, Wikimedia Commons and State Library of Victoria
Front cover Yongyut Kumsri; p 1 Thelma Amaro Vidales; pp 2-3 Harvepino; pp 4-5 Dmytro Pylypenko; pp 6-7 AndreAnita; p 8 I. Noyan Yilmaz; p 9 ugljesa; pp 10-11 Stu Shaw; pp 12-13 Marzolino; p 14 (upper) John King Davis / SLV; p 14 (lower) National Library of Norway / Wikimedia Commons; p 15 (upper) Henry Bowers / Wikimedia Commons; p 15 (lower) Nasjonalbiblioteket / Wikimedia Commons; pp 16-17 gallimaufry; p 18 Yongyut Kumsri; p 19 Durk Talsma; pp 20-21 (upper) I. Noyan Yilmaz; pp 20-21 (lower) Armin Rose; p 22 (upper) Vladislav Gurfinkel; p 22 (lower) Angela N Perryman; p 23 (upper) gary yim; p 23 (lower) Dmytro Pylypenko; p 24 (upper) PIYAPONG THONGDUMHYU; p 24 (lower) Elovich; p 25 Dmytro Pylypenko; p 26 Neale Cousland; p 27 Volodymyr Goinyk; p 28 Dmytro Pylypenko; p 29 MZPHOTO.CZ; p 30 Mogens Trolle; p 31 MZPHOTO.CZ; pp 32-33 Petra Christen; p 34 MZPHOTO.CZ; p 35 fieldwork; p 36 vladsilver; p 37 Jamie Ahmad; pp 38-39 nwdph; p 40 evantravels; p 41 Eduardo Rivero; p 42 Leksele; p 43 Giedriius; p 44 Dmytro Pylypenko; p 45 vladsilver; pp 46-47 vladsilver; p 48 Durk Talsma; p 49 Dmytro Pylypenko; pp 50-51 Ayamik; pp 52-53 Willem Tims; pp 54-55 bruno pagnanelli; p 56 (upper) Bildagentur Zoonar GmbH; p 56 (lower) vinbergv; p 57 TravelMediaProductions; pp 58-59 Stu Shaw; pp 60-61 Durk Talsma; p 64 Kotomiti Okuma; Back cover Volodymyr Goinyk.

FSC® is a non-profit international organisation established to promote the responsible management of the world's forests.

Charles grew up on a hot and dusty farm in the Riverina. He first saw snow on a ski holiday when he was eight years old. He later managed to hurl himself into an embankment, get a concussion and spend several freezing minutes lying in a river. It was at this moment he appreciated just how tough penguins truly are.

Years later, Charles decided to pay tribute to the many plucky creatures that call Antarctica home. He also vowed never to ski into an icy river ever again.

Charles is an editor, proofreader, picture researcher and freelance writer.